Volcanoes of the World™

Mount St. Helens
The Smoking Mountain

Kathy Furgang

The Rosen Publishing Group's
PowerKids Press™
New York

For Jamie

Published in 2001 by The Rosen Publishing Group, Inc.
29 East 21st Street, New York, NY 10010

First Edition

Series and Book Design: Michael Caroleo

Photo Credits: pp. 1,12,19 © Gary Braasch/CORBIS; p. 4 © Galen Rowell/CORBIS; p. 7 Photodisc; p. 8 (illustration) by Michael Caroleo; pp. 11, 15 © CORBIS; p. 16 (top) © David Muench/CORBIS; p. 16 © Roger Ressmeyer/CORBIS; p. 20 © Charles Mauzy/CORBIS.

Furgang, Kathy.
    Mt. St. Helens : the smoking mountain / by Kathy Furgang.— 1st ed.
        p. cm.— (Volcanoes of the world)
    Includes index.
    ISBN 0-8239-5660-1 (alk. paper)
    1. Saint Helens, Mount (Wash.)—Juvenile literature. 2. Volcanoes—Washington (State)—Juvenile literature. [1.Saint Helens, Mount (Wash.) 2. Volcanoes.] I. Title: Mount Saint Helens. II. Title.

QE523.S23 F87 2000
551.21'09797'84—dc21   00-028585

Manufactured in the United States of America

Contents

Mount St. Helens and Mount Rainier (shown in the background), are both part of a group of dangerous volcanoes known as The Ring of Fire.

Mount St. Helens

In the northwest corner of the United States, there is a group of mountains called the Cascade Mountain Range. These mountains stretch from Canada to California. In the middle of the mountain range, in the state of Washington, there is a beautiful mountain called Mount St. Helens. Native Americans who lived in the area hundreds of years ago called the mountain "smoking mountain." They called it that because this mountain is a volcano. From time to time, a volcano like Mount St. Helens sends off a violent explosion of rock, smoke, and **ash** into the air. Volcanoes are a reminder of how powerful nature can be.

The Layers of the Earth

Earth is made up of three layers. The top layer is called the **crust**. This is the outer layer, where we live. Miles (km) below the crust is a layer called the **mantle**. It is so hot in the mantle that rock melts and forms a thick liquid called **magma**. The center of Earth is called the **core**. It is made of solid iron, hot liquid iron, and other **elements**. A volcano is created when magma from Earth's mantle explodes up through the crust.

Crust

Core

Mantle

Earth's crust varies from five miles (8 km) thick to about 25 miles (40 km) thick.
The crust is usually very thick under mountains and thinner under the ocean.

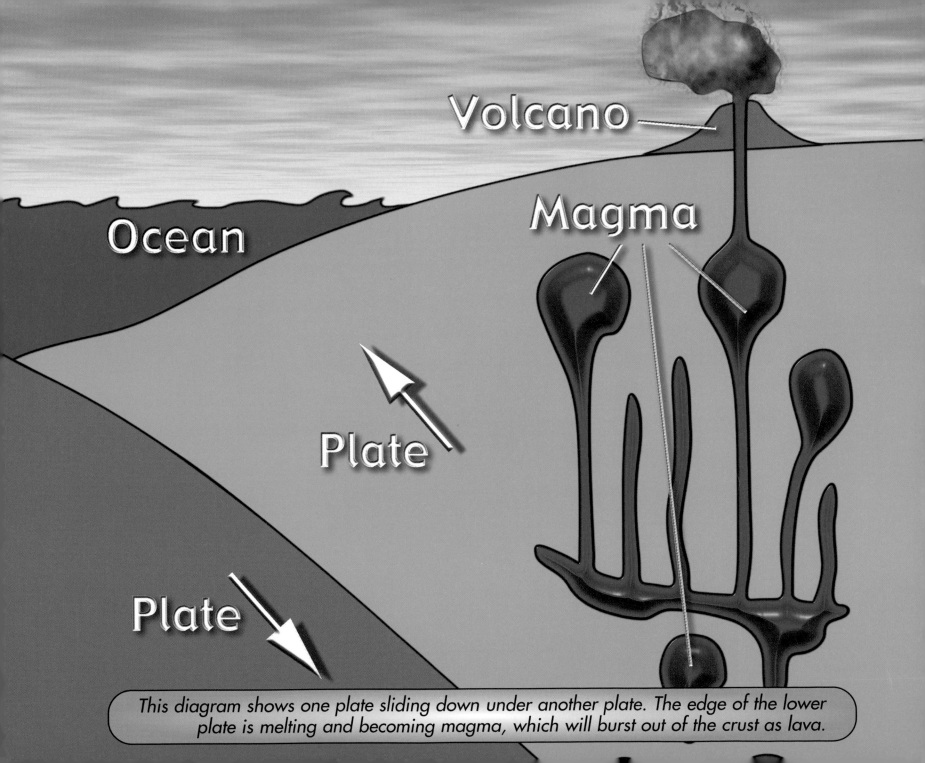

Volcano

Magma

Ocean

Plate

Plate

This diagram shows one plate sliding down under another plate. The edge of the lower plate is melting and becoming magma, which will burst out of the crust as lava.

How Volcanoes Grow

Earth's crust is made up of large sections called **plates**. The plates are moving all the time, even though we can't feel them. Sometimes when two plates bump into one another, one of the plates is pushed down below the crust into the mantle. When this happens, the edge of the plate that is being pushed down melts and becomes magma. The hot magma floats back up to the crust and bursts out. This is called an **eruption**. Once magma comes out of the crust it is called **lava**.

An eruption may also happen when two plates move away from one another, making a space for magma to come to the surface. This happens mostly under the oceans.

9

A Changing Mountain

Mount St. Helens is a **stratovolcano**. A stratovolcano is formed over long periods of time. It is formed by lava from eruptions. The lava hardens in the shape of a cone or a high dome. Mount St. Helens is a mountain made entirely of lava and ash. Volcanic eruptions have changed the shape of the mountain over time. There were many eruptions of Mount St. Helens in the 1800s. After 1857, the mountain was quiet and many people visited it to hike and have fun. Then in 1980, a violent explosion showed just how powerful Mount St. Helens really is. The eruption blasted off more than 1,000 feet (305 m) of the mountain!

This is an image of Mount St. Helens taken from the sky after the 1980 eruption. The dark part is the crater formed by the eruption.

This photograph shows volcanologists at work on Mount St. Helens.
Volcanology is an exciting, but dangerous, science.

Knowing When Danger May Strike

Scientists who study volcanoes are called **volcanologists**. They can sometimes **predict** when a volcano may erupt. They could not predict that Mount St. Helens would erupt on May 18, 1980, but they were very close. There were hundreds of **earthquakes** in the surrounding area between March and May of 1980. That was a clue that the volcano was going to erupt soon. Volcanologists also measure changes in a volcano's height in order to tell what is going on inside the volcano. One part of Mount St. Helens rose and swelled 85 feet (26 m) in the month before the eruption! Volcanologists also test **gases** in the air around the opening of the volcano. Changes in the gases mean that magma is rising in the volcano.

13

Eruption

The largest known explosion of an American volcano came on May 18, 1980, at 8:32 A.M. After months of warning signs, Earth let out a giant explosion from the top of the snow-covered Mount St. Helens. Steam, ash, and gases were blown 12 miles (19.3 km) into the air. The top of the mountain was blasted away, creating a **crater** on the side of the mountain. The eruption killed 57 people and all plant and animal life within an area of 70 square miles (181 sq.km) around the volcano. Ash and rock covered everything as far away as Portland, Oregon!

The eruption of Mount St. Helens on May 18, 1980, was the worst volcanic disaster in the history of the United States.

These photographs show Mount St. Helens before and after the eruption of May 1980. In the bottom photo, the lake is full of dead trees that were carried off the mountain by mudslides.

Mudslides and Falling Ash

It only took minutes for the north side of the snowcapped Mount St. Helens to blow apart. The breaking apart of the mountain caused some of the largest landslides ever recorded. Hot lava melted the snow off the top of the mountain. The melted snow and lava mixed with dirt, ash, and rock to form huge mudslides. Some of the mudslides were as high as a six-story building and moved more than 90 miles (145 km) per hour! The eruption also spread hot ash into the air. In some cities near Mount St. Helens ash fell from the sky and covered everything. The ash in the air above these cities made it dark, even in the middle of the day.

Periods of Activity

Before 1980, Mount St. Helens had not erupted since 1857. The mighty volcano had been sleeping for 123 years! It is normal for volcanoes like Mount St. Helens to go through active periods. During an active period, a volcano erupts more often than usual. A 26-year active period ended for Mount St. Helens in 1857. Just small amounts of steam came from the volcano in 1898, 1903, and 1921. The eruption of 1980 started another active period for Mount St. Helens. The active period lasted for about 10 years with many smaller eruptions. Scientists were able to predict almost every eruption several days to several weeks before it happened. The active period ended in 1990.

Between 1980 and 1990 Mount St. Helens erupted at least 21 more times. All of these eruptions were smaller than the eruption of May 18, 1980. This picture shows an eruption that happened on July 22, 1980.

The trees killed in the eruption of Mount St. Helens will rot and make the soil better for the new plants that are beginning to grow.

Return of Wildlife

The eruption of 1980 caused a lot of damage to the area around the volcano. Over time, however, life began to return to the area. The lava and ash around volcanoes have gases and **minerals** in them that are good for the soil and that help things grow. A plant called fireweed was one of the first plants to start growing on the mountain again. Fireweed seeds put out long roots that can reach through the ash to the soil below. Once the plants began to grow again, the animals returned to the area to live. Deer and elk stirred the ash with their hooves. This spread more seeds around and helped new plants to grow. Today, plants and animals are still returning to Mount St. Helens as the mountain heals.

A National Monument

In the early 1980s, thousands of people visited the area around Mount St. Helens to see the damage the volcano had caused. In 1982, President Ronald Reagan allowed 110,000 acres (44,515 hectares) around the volcano to be set aside for Mount St. Helens National Volcanic Monument. The park has a visitor's center, hiking trails, campgrounds, and picnic areas. Mountain climbers have been allowed to climb to the top of the mountain since 1986. Scientists continue to work hard to track changes that might predict future dangers and eruptions. For now, though, the beautiful Mount St. Helens is quiet and peaceful.

22

Glossary

ash (ASH) Tiny pieces of rock that shoot out of a volcano during an eruption.

core (KOHR) The hot center of Earth that is made of liquid and solid iron and other elements.

crater (KRAY-tehr) A hole in the ground that is shaped like a bowl.

crust (KRUST) The top layer of Earth, where we live.

earthquakes (URTH-kwayks) Movements or shakings of Earth.

elements (EH-lih-mentz) The basic matter that all things are made of.

eruption (eh-RUP-shun) The explosion of gases, smoke, or lava from a volcano.

gases (GAS-ez) Matter that has no shape or size.

lava (LAH-va) Magma that has broken through Earth's crust.

magma (MAG-mah) Hot liquid rock found in Earth's mantle.

mantle (MAN-tuhl) The layer of Earth made of solid rock and magma.

minerals (MIH-nuh-ralz) Substances found in Earth that are not plants or animals.

plates (PLAYTZ) Large sections of Earth's crust that move and shift over time.

predict (PREE-dikt) To make a guess based on facts or information.

stratovolcano (strah-toh-vohl-KAYH-noh) A volcano that forms when many layers of lava build on top of each other.

volcanologists (vol-kuh-NOH-luh-jists) Scientists who study volcanoes.

23

Index

Web Sites

For more information on volcanoes and Mount St. Helens, check out these Web sites:

http:volcano.und.nodak.edu/vwdocs/msh/
http://vulcan.wr.usgs.gov/Volcanoes/MSH/framework.html
http://vulcan.wr.usgs.gov/ljt_slideset.html